C000058276

Kate Hodges

Wild Words

For Rhona and Colin,
Jeff, Arthur and Dusty

A collection of words from around the world that describe happenings in nature

Kate Hodges
Illustrations by Yang Sio Maan

PORTICO

Introduction

Words bestow power. By giving a tree, an animal or a weather phenomenon a name, we acknowledge its existence and mark its place in the world. Conversely, as those natural phenomena wane or disappear, so the terms needed to describe them gather dust and eventually fade from memory.

Across the world, languages spawn words as they are needed; Scotland has over 400 expressions for snow, while the Malaysian Jahai dialect has a finely calibrated lexicon of terms for smells in nature. If the climate, your culture or your safety when outside demand it, words can convey the tiniest, but most essential detail.

Our appreciation of the natural world can be enhanced through language. Now I'm familiar with the word *smeuse* - a passage beneath a bush or wall worn by the feet and sides of animals - I'll never take a walk in the rolling Sussex countryside that surrounds my town without my eyes scanning the base of hedgerows. We can call nature into being with language and use it to bring the wild world vividly to life. Words deepen our understanding of our environment, as well as allowing us to communicate more powerfully about nature.

Sifting through words from around the world brought the wonders of the planet to my desk. While researching this book, my head took a trip to the furthest, most awe-inspiring corners of the Earth. I voyaged through Chinese caves, gazing in awe at rock formations, shook my head at magically glowing mushrooms, danced with witches across the hills of Germany and watched tiny hummingbirds delicately sipping nectar from trumpet-shaped flowers.

I learned about mysterious natural phenomena such as *mistpoeffers* - the deep booms that echo from sea fog and even confuse scientists - and lost myself in the magical Finnish legends that surround the Northern Lights. I took inspiration from notions of how to experience nature; I'll now take time to indulge in Norwegian *friluftsliv*, which is the notion that there's no better way to enjoy nature than doing something relaxing outside, or I'll justify an afternoon snooze in the sun as experimenting with the Italian art of *meriggiare* or taking an afternoon nap.

More generally, I was wide-eyed at how many of the terms I unearthed represent the fragile relationship between humans and the ecosystem. The Maori practice of using *rāhui* bans to conserve is not only spiritual, but essential in a world where nature is constantly fighting its corner against the resource-stripping human race.

Words help to codify our relationship with the planet and can be political. Projects such as The Human Nature Dictionary, a work to create new words for the way that human activity and nature unintentionally intersect, interact or merge, are finding and sharing language that serves to act as a lexicographical shield against the ravages of humans.

Most inspiringly, words can transport us and can conjure up rainbows of colours, smells, tastes and sounds. A dip into this book and a deep drink of Yang Sio Maan's inspirational illustrations will, I hope, give you a glimpse into different landscapes, allow a peep into cultures beyond your own, and serve as a little window onto the constantly changing, phenomenal beauty of the wild world.

Uitwaaien

(OWT-vye-en)

Dutch, Verb

Uitwaaien means literally 'out-blowing', and the Dutch regard the practice as a near-spiritual cure-all. If you're feeling stressed and need to clear your head, or you've got the dry-skin, sluggish-metabolism, central-heating blues, a brisk jaunt outside in the wind will solve all problems. The Netherlands is known for its big-skied flatlands, so finding a blustery spot is rarely a problem. Whether you choose to wander in deep thought, get your blood pumping with a jog, or just face the wind and grin is up to you. Even five minutes *uitwaaien* in a stiff breeze will whisk away the cobwebs and leave you refreshed and ready to take on the world.

Rāhui

(rah-hoo-ee)

Māori, Noun and verb

Combining the practical with the sacred, *rāhui* is the Māori practice
of conserving resources through prohibition. If a field is exhausted,
a *rāhui* - or a temporary ban or restriction - on planting crops will
allow it to recover. When a river is over-fished, a period of prohibition
will encourage wildlife to flourish. A *rāhui* may also be placed out
of respect, to mark the site of a death or to make a political point.
The orders are marked by ceremony and incantations and are often
physically represented by a post, known as a *pou rāhui*, while
some *rāhui* are now set down in law.

Mångata

(mo-an-gaa-tah)

Swedish, Noun

Mångata means the silvery path that the moon's reflection makes on water. The word combines the Swedish words *måne* (moon) and *gata* (street), summoning up a vivid image. In English, this effect is known as a 'glitter path', a term which also encompasses the same phenomenon when caused by the sun. Sailors will use the *mångata* to help navigate; the broader the pale road of light, the bigger the waves are likely to be, thus indicating shallower waters. Look out for one when the moon is bright, the sky is free from clouds and there's a panoramic view of the ocean.

Sugar weather

(shu-garr we-ther)

—————

Canadian English, Noun

Canada's cultural fabric is intertwoven with the maple tree;
its leaf even features on the nation's flag. The country's favourite,
iconic, pancake-topping treat is the syrup made from the tree's sap,
which starts to rise at the start of spring. It's the time of year when the
sun's rays warm your face in the day, but you still need a blanket
on the bed when the temperature dips below zero degrees
centigrade at night. As the sap is tapped, then boiled in heavy
pans, the honeyed smell of syrup drifting from kitchen windows
and curling across still forests gives a name to these fragile,
early spring days: *sugar weather*.

Oubaitori 桜梅桃李

(oh-buy-toe-ree)

Japanese, Idiom

This four-character idiom is made up of the kanji characters for a quartet of trees famous for their beautiful blossom: cherry (桜), plum (梅), peach (桃) and Japanese plum (李). Cherries bloom boldly and beautifully in the spring, the plum in late winter. Peaches are said to ward off evil and promote a long life, while Japanese plums are associated with perseverance. According to the 12th-century Buddhist priest Nichorin, "Cherry, plum, peach and damson blossoms all have their own qualities" (*Gosho Zenshu* - a compilation of all Nichorin's works), and *oubaitori* expresses this idea. Just like these fragile blooms with their delicate but distinct characteristics, everyone has their own, unique personality. We shouldn't spend our lives comparing ourselves with others, but treasure what makes us an individual.

Akua

(ah-koo-ah)

Hawaiian, Noun

The Hawaiian language has a name for every day of the lunar cycle
- 30 different terms - from *hilo* (the faintest thread) through *mōhalu*
(to blossom) to *hua* (egg or fruit). *Akua* is the second of the nights
of the four fullest moons, and its name means god or goddess. Its fat,
creamy light was traditionally good for fishing, a night when gods
welcomed offerings in return for a bounteous catch; one of the most
important periods of the month. The number of names for the
waxing and waning moon reflected its significance to the country's
fishermen and navigators; the cycles affect the tides, harvests and
planting. Hawaii's ancient calendar was even based on the rotation
of the satellite around the earth, and counts nights rather than days.
Their 29-and-a-bit-day lunar month was divided into three *anahulu*
(each *anahulu* signifies a period of ten days/ten nights) that matched
the phases of the moon, compared to the West's roughly 30-day
month, which is divided into seven-day weeks.

Ag borradh

(egg-borrar)

Irish Gaelic, Noun

Colourful Irish writer, John O'Donahue, joyously translated *ag borradh*
as 'a quivering life about to break forth'. It evokes tumescent bulbs on
the verge of bursting through the earth, sheep's bodies tightening with
lambs, the coy nodding of virginal white snowdrops, and the rude
tang of wild garlic. In Ireland and across the UK, the February 2
festival of Christian Candlemas or Pagan Imbolc marks and
welcomes these first shoots of spring and the growing strength of the
sun; both important milestones for those who relied on the soil and
agriculture to survive. The season's wheel is turning,
and bounteous spring is set to return.

Sirimiri/Chipi chipi/Rimjhim

(si-ri-mi-ri)/(chipee-chipee)/(rim-jim)

Spanish/Mexican/Sanskrit, Noun

The barely there sibilance of light rain lends itself to ear-tickling
onomatopoeia and a rhythmical repeat in many languages.
Sirrrri mirrrri, chiiiiipi chiiiiiipi, rimmmmmjhimmmmmm.
The words conjure up images of tiny droplets speckling hot
rooftops, whispery showers tickling the leaves at the very top
of trees, or of waking up to the softest whisper of weather outside;
often a welcome relief from baking heat. Is it fog? Or is it rain?
Its danker, more miserable English cousin is known in the
south-west of the country as *mizzle:* half mist, half drizzle.

Murr-ma

(mer-ma)

Wagiman, Verb

The Wagiman language is near-extinct and is spoken by only
a handful of elderly people in Australia's Northern Territory. It's
expected to die out over the next few decades, which is a tragedy,
as this complex, rich, ancient tongue is quite distinct from others in
the region. *Murr-ma* is the word for the act of searching for something
in the water with only your feet. It conjures up images of waves warm
enough to paddle in, of shallow lagoons and summer fishing trips.
The word ebbs and flows around your mouth like little eddies of salty
water around your toes. But what will you find as you feel around?
A shell? Treasure? A confused crab?

Gluggaveður

(glook-ah-vay-therr)

Icelandic, Noun

Translated literally, *gluggaveður* means 'window weather'. It describes the kind of day that looks beautiful when viewed from a cosy seat indoors, but is not so pleasant to spend any amount of time in. A snowstorm is the perfect example; a scene from a fairytale when viewed from a warm room with a smug mug of coffee, but once you've pulled on your warmest clothes and ventured outside, a soggy, freezing nightmare. The word encapsulates the wisdom of those raised in fierce climates; never underestimate the power of the weather and, if you do venture into a bracing day, prepare yourself thoroughly.

Beija-flor

(bay-jar florr)

Portuguese, Noun

Tiny and jewel-like, hummingbirds are almost more insect than bird,
their wings creating the buzz that gives them their English name.
Surprisingly speedy - they can travel at up to 45mph - they flit from
flower to flower, using their long, tube-like tongues to feed;
as they have to replenish every 10-15 minutes, that's thousands of
visits a day. Portuguese speakers call them *beija-flor*, a term almost as
exquisite as the creatures themselves. It links *beija* (kiss) and
flor (flower) to describe the dainty manner in which the
hummingbird feeds on nectar.

Soseol 소살

(soh-si-al)

Korean, Noun

소살 *Soseol* is the day when Koreans open their arms, throw back their heads and wait expectantly for the first snowfall of winter. The word means 'little snow' and the predictable climate of Korea means that November 22 or 23 is the day when the first flakes are expected to fall. Romantics believe that if you're with your sweetheart as the first flurries begin, you'll stay together forever, and Korean films and TV shows will often feature a scene in which two lovers kiss as the landscape is blanketed in white. Others say that if you make a wish on *Soseol* it will come true.

Akash Ganga आकाशगंगा

(akash-ganj-ah)

Sanskrit, Noun

Sanskrit is one of the most beautiful languages in the world; sacred, soothing and able to express complex philosophical notions elegantly. As you would expect from a dialect that poetically captures the greatest natural marvels, it has ten names for the Milky Way. Among them are *Maṃdākinī* (the calm or unhurried one) and *Akash Ganga*, which is used across many Indian languages and means literally 'the Ganges of the sky'. *Akash* means sky, while *Ganga* refers to the sacred River Ganges, which is broad like the Milky Way.

Mistpoeffer

(mist-perfer)

Dutch, Noun

Boooooom. Booooooooom. A *mistpoeffer* (or *mistpouffer*) is the mysterious, deep, thumping sound that echoes from fog in coastal regions or over lakes and rivers. Boooooom. There's no scientific explanation for the worldwide phenomenon; theories range from solar winds to gas bubbles, underground earthquakes to meteors. These unexplainable thunderous rumbles can be plate-rattlingly loud. In Japan they're known as *uminari* (cries from the ocean), in France as *canons de mer* (guns of the sea) and in English-speaking regions as *skyquakes*. In 1851, American author, James Fenimore Cooper, described the *Seneca guns* of the New Jersey Catskill Mountains as "resembling the explosion of a heavy piece of artillery, that can be accounted for by none of the known laws of nature."

Ghurfa غرفة

(goo-hr-far)

Arabic, Noun

The Arabic language crystallised in parts of the world covered in arid desert. So it's not surprising that there is a word for 'the amount of water that can be held in one hand'; *ghurfa* means literally 'hollow of the hand'. It appears in the Quranic verse, "Indeed Allah will be testing you with a river. So whoever drinks his fill from it is not of me, and whoever does not taste it is indeed of men, excepting one who takes a sip from the hollow of his hand." (Quran, 1: 249)

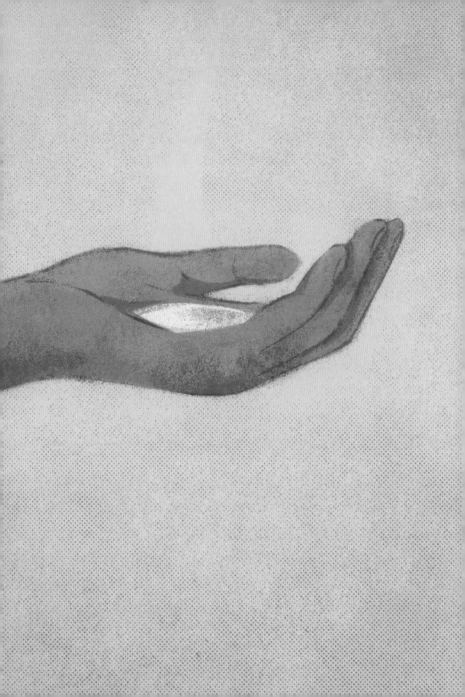

Plaheng plʔɛŋ

(pla-engh)

Jahai, Noun

Language adapts to the needs of those who speak it. English speakers have thousands of words for colours, but very few for smells. However, the indigenous Malaysian dialect of Jahai, spoken mainly by those who live in Perak (Malaysia), has more finely calibrated words to describe scents. *Plaheng* (the blood-like smell that attracts tigers) is used to describe the odours of crushed headlice or squirrel's blood. Another word, *chengus* (to have a stinging smell) encompasses the smell of wild mango, ginger roots, bat caves, droppings of bats, smoke and petrol. This precise palette of terms is vital to the Jahai people, who hunt and need to avoid scents that attract dangerous predators such as tigers.

Mono no aware
もののあはれ

(mo-nor nor awarr-ey)

Japanese, Phrase

Every spring, Japan's cherry blossom season brings clouds of fragile
pastel-pink flowers to the country's parks and mountainsides.
Of course, the sight is heart-soaringly gorgeous, but the dazzle
is undercut with a sense of wistfulness that the display is only fleeting,
and that the blossom must brown and fall within weeks.
An understanding of the impermanence of beauty is central to
the concept of *mono no aware* (the sadness of things). This bittersweet
appreciation of the transient nature of perfection can be applied
more widely, to life, ageing and death.

Arc de Sant Martí

(ark duh sant martee)

Catalan, Noun

Before science brought its cool-eyed, logical explanations,
the sight of a multi-coloured arch rising between the clouds must
have seemed near-magical. No wonder there are folktales related
to the phenomenon worldwide. Catalonian legend has it that Sant
Martí, a Catholic warrior saint, played a trick on the devil. Each was
to make a bow across the sky. Sant Martí spun his from glass in seven
bright colours, while the devil used ice to make a smaller, less vivid
version. As the two gazed at their creations, the smaller ice rainbow
melted away. This is said to explain the second rainbow that appears
beside the main attraction. The coloured arch therefore took
its creator's name: *Arc de Sant Martí.*

Alimuóm

(a-lee-moo-om)

Tagalog, Noun

This is the mild smell of soil as the rain hits the ground, specifically sun-warmed earth. The scent holds a near-mystical allure, setting noses a-twitch at the first sight of heavy summer clouds, and, consequently, it's been chased by perfumers eager to capture its elusive, bitter-sweet tang. In Tagalog, the language that forms the basis of the national language of the Philippines, there's an idiom, *mapagsagap ng alimuóm* ('inhaling vapour rising from the ground after the rain'), which has come to mean a gossip. The Filipinos also have a superstition that the smell of *alimuóm* causes stomach ache. The English equivalent, *petrichor*, was coined in the 1960s by two Australian researchers.

Crepuscular

(crepp-usk-u-lah)

English, Adjective

After the sun dips below the horizon, its pink and orange light
continues to flatter the landscape before fading slowly into inky blue.
These gentle, woozy colours tempt out those animals that live in the
half-time between day and night, and these creatures are *crepuscular*
(from the Latin *crepusculum*, meaning 'twilight'). Barn owls flap
banshee-like between the skeletons of trees, glow-worms dot
luminously in bushes, rats scurry purposefully along pavements.
Those who come out solely in the evening are *vespertine*, while
early risers are *matutinal*.

Waldeinsamkeit

(valt-ine-sam-kite)

German, Noun

The peaceful feeling of wandering alone in a forest might seem very particular; it needs nine English words to describe it. However, the German language has just one word for it, a compound of *wald* (wood) and *einsamkeit* (solitude). The practice of losing oneself in a wood is regarded by Germans as being a healthy, inexpensive route to mindfulness. The term conjures up images of being dwarfed by tall firs, of staring up into a thick canopy of stars, or of the vista across a lush, wooded valley. It evokes the smell of damp pines and mushrooms and the sounds of twigs broken by scuttling creatures. More widely, it sums up the sense of flying solo in nature, of being alone with your thoughts and plans, or of contemplating your insignificance in the infinite cosmos.

Will-o'-the-Wisp

(will-oh thur wisp)

English, Noun

These ghostly, floating, blue balls of flame bob over marshes or flicker over moorland. In the UK and parts of America, they're believed to be malevolent spirits tempting unwitting travellers to a watery doom. In Mexico, they are *brujas* (witches), in Columbia *La Candileja* is the ghost of an evil grandmother, while in Brazil, they represent *boi-tatá*, the 'fiery serpent'. Across Scandinavia and northern Europe, the lights are believed to indicate the site of buried or sunken fairy treasure that might be taken only when the fire is burning. Scientists would have you believe that the phenomenon is caused either by the spontaneous combustion of phosphine, diphosphane and methane (marsh gas) or bioluminescent gases but, intriguingly, even they aren't sure.

Godhuli गोधूलि

(god-hooli)

Bengali, Noun

This almost filmic word means 'dust of the cows'. It describes the time
of day when the sun sets and the herds return home from
a day's grazing, their hooves raising dust into the pinky, early evening
air. The word is derived from the Sanskrit *go* (cow) and *dhuli* (dust);
the reference to cows, revered and regarded as symbols of life in
Hindu cultures, reflects the magical, sacred nature of this time
of day. It's deeply evocative; yellow-orange light, clouds billowing
from the baked earth, the smell of animals, the sound
of lazy hooves, the shouts of herders mingled with
the final warm rays of sun.

Meriggiare

(merry-JAR-ay)

Italian, Verb

The luxuriant pleasures of relaxing at noon, usually in a shady spot on a sunny day, are summed up by this Italian word. Derived from *meriggio* meaning 'midday', it conjures up the intense heat of the overhead sun and the respite given by a canopy of leaves or a parasol. Formerly associated with the much-needed afternoon rest taken by farm workers, it's now just as likely to refer to taking time out to drink a long, cool glass of something sparkling with a book in your hand. More common in verse than everyday prose, the word is the title of a famous poem by Italian writer, Eugenio Montale.

Dalalæða

(da-lar-leth-err)

Icelandic, Noun

Iceland is wreathed in myths; sneaky trolls, gods who wielded giant hammers, and goddesses who ride chariots pulled by cats across the night sky. Their stories played out among the geysers, fjords and mountains of Scandinavia, while the *dalalæða* swirled around their feet. Literally meaning 'valley sneak', this waist-deep fog creeps into gorges, slowly engulfing peaks. If the conditions are right – the phenomenon often occurs on a calm night after a warm day - as it crests *kletturs* (rocks) the *dalalæða* will pour over the edge like a misty waterfall. Dramatic, magical and ethereal, and a sight to make the senses roar.

Hexenringe

(hex-en-rin-ge)

German, Noun

Every year, on Walpurgisnacht (April 30), the witches of Germany
whisk into the air on their broomsticks to gather on the highest peak
of the Harz mountains, the Brocken. There, they dance wildly with
the devil. The crones' relentless feet wear circles in the ground called
hexenringe (witch's rings) - *fairy rings* in English. Across Europe, these
patterns left by mushrooms are associated with the supernatural;
the Dutch believe the devil kept his milk churn in them, Austrians
believe that they were burned into the ground by dragons' tails, and
the British say that if you enter a fairy ring, you'll be condemned
to dance with the little folk until you go mad or die of exhaustion.

Skábma

(skarrb-ma)

Sámi, Noun

The Sámi people inhabit the northernmost parts of Scandinavia
and the far west of Russia. As they live so close to the North Pole,
for over a month each winter the sun doesn't rise above the horizon;
this is the polar night or 'days without shadow'. But rather than
dreading this period of darkness, the Sámi embrace it. *Skábma* is
a time to cosy up by the fire with family, to knit, tell stories and
laugh. It's a period to feel no guilt about doing little except to craft
and pickle, to light candles and luxuriate indoors, or to head outside
for cross-country skiing and ice-hole fishing. The sun may have gone,
but its light still dances on the clouds, and reflects on the snow,
making this the most magical time of the year. Slowly, slowly
the full light will return. As the Sámi say, "The day gets longer
one ptarmigan step each day."

Smultronställe

(smul-tron-stellar)

Swedish, Noun

The direct translation of this Swedish word is 'a small remote place where wild strawberries grow'. However, as well as describing a wild, grassy spot thick with the sweet smell of ripening fruit, it has a deeper, almost spiritual resonance. Swedish speakers use it when describing the semi-secret place that makes them happy, whether that be a mountain top, a particular park bench, or even a backstreet in a city. Strawberries, though lovely, are not necessary. It's a concept so embedded in Swedish culture that the country's legendary film director, Ingmar Bergman, made a movie of (nearly) the same name, *Smultronstället*, which referenced both meanings of the word.

Revontulet

(ray-von-tyu-lett)

Finnish, Noun (plural)

The constantly shifting, stratosphere-scraping Northern Lights
are one of the most beautiful sights in the natural world. In Finland,
the phenomenon is known as *revontulet* (fox-fires). Finnish myths tell
that these sheets of rainbow fire were created by *tulikettu*, a magical
fox keenly sought after by hunters. As he bounded across the valleys
of the country, his flaming tail would sweep across the snow, spraying
ice crystals into the sky, and his static-charged fur would
set the heavens on fire. As he touched the mountains, bright sparks
would fly into the night. The ancient Finnish word for 'magic'
was also very similar to 'fox', so some believe that
revontulet means 'spell fires'.

Komorebi 木漏れ日

(kom-or-ray-bee)

Japanese, Noun

If the forest is a cathedral, *komorebi* are the bright shafts of sunlight that shine down through its stained-glass windows. The beams might be awe-inspiring and broad, illuminating whole glades, or silhouetting a magnificent stag. Alternatively, they could be more humble, filtering through leaves and creating a dappled sun dance on the forest floor. Knotted into the word are deeper concepts of the contrast between light and shade, the gentle pull between darkness and positivity, and the privilege of experiencing transient beauty. The practice of *shinrin-yoku* or therapeutic 'forest bathing' is popular in Japan; perhaps *komorebi* serve as the bath bubbles that make these deeply immersive woodland walks even more indulgent. The word is made up of the kanji characters for tree (木), shine through (漏れ), and sun (日).

Matahari

(mat-ar harr-ee)

Malayan and Indonesian, Noun

In many Southeast Asian languages, the word for sun literally means
'eye of the day'. In Thai, it's *tâ* (eye) *wan* (day), in Fijian it's *mata ni siga*
(day's face) and in Malayan and Indonesian, *mata* (eye) *hari* (day).
It's an evocative description, our giver of light, round like an eye,
watching over his charges on the Earth below. Many Westerners
know the term from its adoption as a stage name by Dutch
exotic dancer and World War I German spy,
Margaretha Geertruida Zelle.

Zubato sunce

(zoo-bat-oh sance)

Serbian and many Balkan languages, Noun

A winter's sun might be bright, but its powers to warm you up
are limited. Across the Balkans, this deceptive watery light is
known as *zubato sunce* (sun with big teeth). From inside, the sun looks
inviting, but once you're out, you'll soon realise just how cold the
temperature is. Some say that the word personifies the sun
that gives you frostbite and gnaws off unsuspecting digits.
Others believe that its origins are more similar to the English
'biting cold'. Or perhaps it's more like the wolf in Little Red
Riding Hood, baring his teeth ahead of his deadly,
chilly attack.

Dadirri

(dah-did-ee)

Ngan'gikurunggurr and Ngen'giwumirri, Noun

Finding peace in nature is common across the world, but the practice of entering into the wild and tapping into an inner spring in order to find a deep awareness or *dadirri*, is expressed with a bright clarity by the Aboriginal people who live in the Daly River region of Australia. It's about *listening*, not doing, and is a form of 'tuning in' to the earth's resonances, to the rustling of plants, the hum of insects, and to the stillness of the earth in order to connect with the natural world.

Opplett

(op-let)

Norwegian, Noun

The western coast of Norway has a reputation for rain. In Bergen, annual precipitation is 2,200mm, and in towns at the foot of the hills, it's over 3000mm (London gets around 500-600mm a year and New York 710-1600mm). So little glimpses of sunshine are welcomed with broad smiles. *Opplett* is the word for the breaks between the showers, a few minutes of sun, and Norwegians have become masters of grabbing the opportunity to enjoy those moments. As they like to say, "*Det er opplett ute!*" ("Enjoy the sunshine!"). It's about optimism, a glass half-full attitude, living in the present and taking advantage of the (sometimes brief) good times while you can.

Gökotta

(zho-koh-tar)

Swedish, Noun

The dawn chorus is nature's wake-up call, a twittering, chirping symphony of birds greeting the morning sun. Starting an hour or so before sunrise, it's a way for males to attract females; an impressive singer is likely to make a good mate. In spring, the concert of competing chirrups, songs and squawks is at its most impressive, and in Sweden, there's a rich tradition of rising early to go out into the soft sunrise and listen to the birds. Sweden even has a name for the magical experience: *gökotta* (early morning cuckoo).

Sternschnuppe

(shtairn-shnoop-ah)

German, Noun

No matter which country they're viewed from, shooting stars are
magical, but by the time you've pointed to these streaks of light,
they've faded. Meteors are specks of space dust or small rocks that
burn as they speed through the earth's upper atmosphere. This sweet
German word translates literally as 'smouldering star rubbish'
- *Schnuppe* is from the Middle High German *schnuppe*, meaning snuff
or the charred wick of a candle. Like many people around the world,
Germans believe that falling stars grant wishes, on the condition
you don't tell anyone your secret desire.

Hanyauku

(harn-yoh-ku)

Rukwangali, Verb

Rukwangali is the language spoken by Namibians, and when huge swathes of your country are covered by the Namib Desert, a word that means to walk on tiptoes across hot sand is a vital arrow in your vocabulary quiver. The quick, triple-syllabled *hanyauku* is phonesthemic (its sound suggests a meaning): hop, skip, jump; ouch, eek, ow! It suggests the motions of someone bare-footed tackling an area of scalding-hot beach, possibly resulting in some pain and burned soles. The quandary: to run quickly and carelessly, or to go slower and more gingerly?

Víðsýni

(vith-see-nee)

Icelandic, Adjective

Iceland is a country with relatively few trees, making its dramatic
vistas all the wider and starker; *víðsýni* (wide vision) is the word for
that broad, horizon-to-horizon, panoramic view. Is there a feeling
that beats the giddiness of endorphins that course through your veins
as you turn to take in a spectacular landscape, particularly
after a long, gruelling climb? In addition to the literal meaning,
Icelandic speakers also use the term to mean open-mindedness
or 'wide-visioned'; a quality valued hugely in a country that has
elected young, female Prime Ministers and is spearheading
the global environmental movement.

Pukh Пух

(pukk)

Russian, Noun

It's June. You're in Moscow. And the city is covered in white clouds of poplar seeds, known as *pukh*. Literally meaning 'fluff', this downy 'summer snow' envelopes the city; you'll find *pukh* in your apartment, piled on your car, tangled into your hair, and in every crevice of your body. The seeds are highly flammable, so the drifts can be a safety hazard; *pukh* fires are a real threat, with street posters warning of the dangers. By the end of June, however, the storm has subsided.

The word is also associated with a very famous bear; the Russians know Winnie the Pooh as *Vinni Pukh*.

Murmuration

(murr-murr-a-shun)

English, Noun

Singularly, starlings are chirpy and ubiquitous, but collectively they
weave magic across the sky. Their dusk-and-dawn behaviour seems
almost telepathic; huge flocks, which sometimes number
in the hundreds of thousands, gather to eddy and flow back and
forth, moving as a whole, rapidly changing direction, swooping
and looping. Common across Europe, northern America and the
southern tips of Australasia and Africa, these awe-inspiring displays
take place just before the flock roosts and just after it rises.
Scientists believe that individual birds react lightning-fast to those
closest to them, co-ordinating these flying flash mobs on the wing.
The enormous gatherings discourage predators, provide a forum
for communication and help the birds keep warm. They also
provide one of the greatest spectacles of the natural world;
arrive about an hour before the sun sets or rises to enjoy
a front-row seat.

Yowe-tremmle

(yow trem-el)

Scottish, Noun

In Scotland, there's often a spell of cold weather in June after the sheep's thick fleeces have been shorn. The flocks shiver, bleating and skinny like winter swimmers. The name for this regular burst of chilly weather is *yowe-tremmle*, literally 'ewe tremble' in old Scottish dialect. Across the world, people recognise weather patterns, which they codify with names or in verse. The Scots also have the three-day *gowk's storm* which arrives with the cuckoo, while the cold weather that arrives around May 1 is called the *gab o' Mey*. Some weather sequences are more complex, determined by the conditions on a given date. In the UK, if Candlemas (February 2) is sunny, the rest of the winter will be harsh, but if it's cold and wet, then the weeks ahead will be easier. The American Groundhog Day (also on February 2), which also predicts the ferocity of the rest of the winter, has its roots in this tradition.

Hoppípolla

(hoppy pollar)

Icelandic, Verb

This compound word, which describes jumping joyfully in puddles, was coined by the band Sigur Rós from the phrase *hoppa í polla* (hopping into puddles) and became the title of the band's second single, which was released in 2005. Most of the band's lyrics are in Icelandic, but some are in a 'language' they've invented called *Vonlenska* (Hopelandic). It may be an invented word, but it's much needed; who doesn't enjoy leaping and splashing in pools of water? The perfect example of language evolving, *hoppípolla* may even become part of the everyday Icelandic lexicon.

Dumbledore

(dum-bl-dorr)

English, Noun

Short, fat and hairy, with stubby little wings, bumblebees are not the most elegant of creatures. Their heavy, clumsy flight, content buzz and rotund appearance gave them their name, bumblebee, but also inspired an 18th-century term, *dumbledore*. The term is so evocative, it was borrowed by JK Rowling for her Harry Potter series; she christened the much-loved headmaster of Hogwarts, Albus Dumbledore. She once said, "Because [he] is very fond of music, I always imagined him as sort of humming to himself a lot."

Porosha пороша

(porr-osh-ar)

Russian, Noun

Russia has at least 100 words for snow, with many more regional variations, from the crystalline *tselyak*, which means 'flawless snow with no trails or marks', to the grimmer *slyakot*, which is 'wet snow mushed with mud'. *Porosha* is one of the most heart-stopping kinds of snow - the pristine variety that has fallen silently on a windless night, pure but for the odd bird or animal trail. It's the kind of white stuff that prompts excited cries, a rush to pull on coats and boots, and joyful whoops as the neighbourhood runs outside for snowball fights and sledging.

Dauwtrappen

(dow-trappen)

Dutch, Verb

The Dutch have a tradition that on Ascension Day, which falls forty days after Easter Sunday, they get up early in order to hike or go for a bicycle ride. The practice of *dauwtrappen* (dew-treading) dates back into the distant past when people would wake at 3am in order to run barefoot into the wet grass and dance to celebrate spring and new life, and reap the health benefits of the tiny drops of water suspended on blades of grass. Many cultures around the world praise the curative properties of spring dew; in the UK, it's said that if you wash your face in the wet grass on May 1, you'll have a flawless complexion for the next year.

Sēnlín 森林

(sen-lin)

Mandarin, Noun

Chinese can be a beautifully literal language, visually as well as
aurally. The character 木 (*mù*) means timber in modern Chinese
but, in the classic language, referred to a tree. So, of course, if you
put two of these characters together 林 (*lín*) it means a grove or
man-made forest, using three 森 (*sēn*) refers to a more natural forest
that is dense enough to block natural sunlight, while five create
森林 (*sēnlín*), which means a dark, large forest.

Hiraeth

(here-eyeth)

Welsh, Noun

Hiraeth is homesickness, but homesickness on a vertiginous scale. It's a melancholy ache for your spiritual home, a nostalgia for a place perhaps only found in memories, a yearning for a past that no longer exists, or that perhaps never existed. *Hiraeth* courses through the veins of Welsh people like a mountain stream flows through a valley. However, this gentle, whispery word not only evokes a state of mind, but also the rugged physicality and myth-soaked, misty sweep of Wales. It summons a longing for the drizzled slate and waterfall landscapes, red kites and sleeping kings.

Calabobos

(CAL-a-bob-oss)

Spanish, Noun

Old man weather has some sneaky tricks up his sleeve. The northern shores of Spain are regularly misted by a fine, continuous drizzle, so ethereal it barely registers. Why bother wearing a coat? It's hardly rain. Wouldn't an umbrella be overkill? However, after spending a few minutes in it, those who follow that logic are soaked to the skin and feeling very sheepish. It's named after those naive enough to underestimate its power to drench: *calabobos* (fool soaker).

Poronkusema

(porron-kuss-emma)

Finnish, Noun

The Finnish lexicon contains over a thousand reindeer-related words, reflecting the importance of the animal to their culture, their lives and in their history. *Leami* means a short, fat female reindeer, while *busat* describes a bull with only one testicle. An archaic unit of measurement, *poronkusema* (reindeer's peed by) is the distance a reindeer can comfortably travel before needing a break to have a wee - about 7.5km. Another, somewhat idiosyncratic, unit of distance used by the Sámi is *peninkulma*, which is the name for the distance a barking dog can be heard in still air (about 10km).

Erumpent

(ee-rum-pent)

English, Adjective

The kind of word that will make you blush without quite knowing why, *erumpent* describes the bursting forth of plants, buds and fungi spores, particularly in spring. Used in the thigh-slapping 17th century, it's as if rampant, rump and erect had an orgy and produced the baby with the very rudest name. It's something you can imagine a ruddy-faced town mayor declaiming on May Day in a speech that describes both the countryside and the effect the blushing girls lined up hoping to become May Queen have on the townsmen's trousers. *Erumpent* was borrowed by JK Rowling for the name of the rhinoceros-like beast in her Harry Potter books.

Upepo

(uu-pe-poh)

Swahili, Noun

In the endless heat and humidity of Kenya and Tanzania, a light breeze brings sweet relief. *Upepo* means a wind, and *kupunga upepo* means to get a blessed breath of fresh air. It's something to wish for, rather than the harsh *baridi upepo* (cold wind). For Swahili speakers, the word conjures up images of chilling out on white-sanded beaches, hair lightly ruffled, or lying in a boat being rocked gently by a sea breeze.

Éloize

(el-was)

Acadian French, Noun

Éloize means 'heat lightning' in Acadian French, a language that is spoken in parts of Canada. Rather beautifully, the word looks like the phenomenon it names, the Z flashing across the page like a thunderbolt. Heat lightning is the term used for those eerie faint flashes on the horizon that have no accompanying sound of thunder. Although some believe that these seemingly silent storms are caused by the heat, the lack of sound is purely due to their distance from the viewer. They're associated with warm, clear nights, as that's when there are likely to be more potential viewers out in the pleasant weather.

Cynefin

(cuh-ner-vin)

Welsh, Noun

Coarsely translated, this Welsh word means 'habitat', but its significance is much more complex and nuanced. The word originated from a farming term for 'demand paths' - those tracks worn by animals' feet - and describes the environment in which someone was raised and, therefore, where they feel most at home. Over the years, it has come to mean more, conveying the complex relationship between the nature of your upbringing and the place in which your formative years were spent. It's that place you feel you ought to be, your spiritual home.

Flori de gheață

(floor-ee day ghee-artar)

Romanian, Noun

When it's bitterly cold and your windows are single-glazed, keeping the weather outside and the warmth in can be a battle. But perhaps it's worth braving the chill if, when you awake, the panes are etched with gorgeous frosty patterns. Romanian speakers know them as *flori de gheață* (ice flowers) because of their fractal, fern-like appearance. They are formed when water vapour lurking inside the house condenses and freezes onto glass, a material that conducts heat much faster than the walls surrounding it.

Yambi

(yam-bee)

Manchu, Noun

Manchu was once the national language of China, but now fewer than a thousand people speak it. However, its script is regarded as 'silky and graceful', and it is said that writing in it is more akin to painting. *Yambi* means 'to rise' and is used to describe the evening vapours that come during the period of calm just after sunset. The image of steam rising lazily from fields as the world winds down is as smooth and soothing as the word itself.

Tükörsima

(took-er shee-ma)

Hungarian, Noun

Literally meaning 'mirror-flat', *tükörsima* describes the calmest of waters. Living in a landlocked country, the people of Hungary look to lakes and ponds rather than the ocean for solace and recreation, and Europe's largest freshwater lake, Lake Balaton, is one of the most famous and popular beauty spots in Hungary. On a very still day, when the water lies undisturbed by wind, swimmers or birds, it's like glass, reflecting cloud-free blue sky and the surrounding gently sloping hills. The shimmering sound of the word echoes its meaning, and even murmuring it to yourself brings a sense of peace.

Zhōngrǔ-shí 钟乳石

(zong-ru-shee) and Shí-sǔn 石笋 (shee-sun)

Mandarin, Nouns

Unlike in English, in Mandarin there is no confusion between stalactite and stalagmite. The translation of stalagmite is 'rock bamboo shoot', while stalactite is, ahem, 'hanging-bell nipple rock'. The Mandarin word for stalactite references an instrument that is shaped like a bell with very distinctive protrusions, while the 'rock bamboo shoot' conjures up a distinctive image of a burgeoning plant. These tooth-like protrusions that hang down and grow upwards in caves are formed from calcite, a mineral that is left behind by dripping water. There is an old saying in China that claims, "the consistent water can drop through the stone", but stalagmites and stalactites are monuments that suggest consistent water can also form a stone.

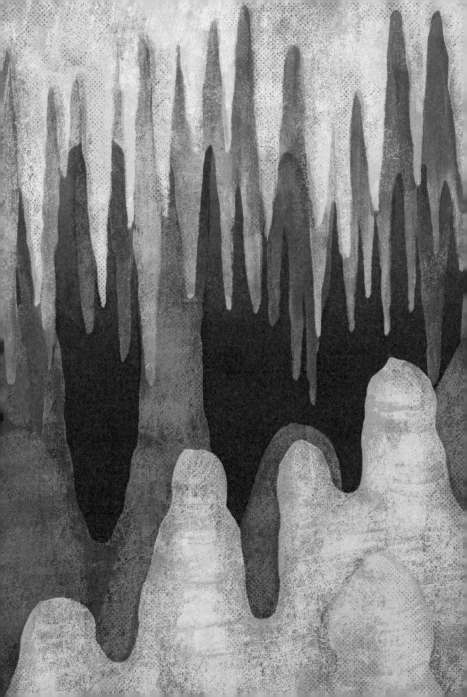

Qanisqineq

(kkan-is-kkin-ekk)

Yupik, Noun

The hoary idea that there are fifty (or a hundred, or more) Eskimo-Aleut language words for snow has been drifting around since the early part of the 20th century. The theory has been repeated until it became fact - Kate Bush even released an album called *50 Words For Snow* - then debunked and rebunked over the last few decades. The problem with establishing how many words for snow exist in this group of languages is setting definitions. What dialects are being included? Are compound words acceptable? And where does the definition of 'snow' end? *Qanisqineq* is one of the genuine root words, and it's rather beautiful. It's the Yupik - the Inuit language spoken in parts of south-west Alaska - word for fallen snow floating on water. Today, snow on water might be dangerous for boats, jamming their motors, but historically, hunters melted the fresh snow to use as drinking water.

Lieko

(lee-ay-ko)

Finnish, Noun

Legend has it that there are ten trees in Finland for every person in the world. In the past, these forests were spiritually important; groves were places where gods were worshipped. Even today the country's capital city, Helsinki, is brimming with wild woods and nature reserves. So it's no wonder there are hundreds of tree-related words in Finnish. Deliciously precise, the old Finnish word *lieko* means a tree that has fallen, often into a lake or marsh. It's evocative; the skeleton yellowing through leafy water, and a little sad; this once mighty warrior felled and left to rot out of sight in the cold depths.

Fox-fire

(fox fy-ar)

English, Noun

In a pre-scientific world, the sight of mushrooms glowing in the dark would have been mystifying, and probably ascribed to magic. No wonder fungi have so much superstition and folklore swirling around them. This other-worldly phenomenon of bioluminescence was first noted by Aristotle, who described a light 'cold to the touch'. In the UK, glimmering mushrooms are rarely seen, but worldwide, they are more common, shining eerily in forests and with names such as *jack o'lanterns* and *bleeding fairy helmets*. In English, this incandescence is known as *fox-fire*, thought to come from the old French word *fol* (false).

Volta

(VOL-tar)

Greek, Noun

Picture a balmy summer evening, the sun setting lazily over the sea.
Lights twinkle, people stroll along, greeting each other. In Greece,
a walk like this is known as a *volta*. A gentle promenade rather
than a hike, a Sunday outing rather than a weekday commute.
The expression *pame volta* means literally 'let's take a turn'. It's an
enjoyable way to enjoy nature and get some very light exercise
with no stressful expectations. Sociable, scenic and relaxed.
What a perfect way to unwind at the end of a day.

Eglė

(egg-ahl)

Lithuanian, Noun

According to Lithuanian legend, *Eglė* is the Queen of Serpents, the heroine of a fairytale that includes snakes that shape-shift into princes, undersea kingdoms, revenge and bloody murder. At the climax of the story, lost in furious grief for her beloved husband, *Eglė* transforms her family into trees - her sons into an oak, an ash and a birch, and her daughter into a trembling aspen - then turns herself into a spruce. Lithuanians associate spruce with witches, death and misfortune; it's still customary to place twigs from the tree on graves.

Stjerneklart

(styern-er-klart)

Norwegian, Noun

The sight of an arching, star-hung night sky might be one of the most awe-inspiring and humbling views nature has to offer. The endless black of night, illuminated only by infinite stars, can be almost too much to bear. With its low-density population and wide fjords, Norway has thousands of square miles of country that's perfect for stargazing, so it's little wonder that the Norwegian word *stjerneklart* (starlit) encapsulates this feeling of majesty, wonder and stark beauty with such precision.

Feefle

(fee-ful)

Scottish, Noun

The Eskimo-Aleut languages may have 50 words for snow
(see page 122), but researchers at the University of Glasgow claim the
Scots language has over 421. From *flindrikin* for a light shower to
snaw-broo for melted slush, *gramschoch* for the conditions just before a
storm, and *skelf* meaning snowflake, there are hundreds of blizzard-
related terms. Perhaps the most evocative is *feefle* (swirls of snow);
its near-Dickensian name conjures the gusts of flakes that eddy
in random bursts from behind brickwork or blow around the base
of pine trees. Rather prosaically, its origins lie in *feef*
(a whiff of an unpleasant smell).

Rudenėja

(roo-den-ay-HA)

Lithuanian, Verb

This Lithuanian word might be baldly translated as 'becoming autumnal', but has a far deeper resonance. It describes the turning of the seasons as lazy, balmy, summer days sharpen into something leaner and crisp; a time when the edges of green leaves crackle orange, the smell of bonfires hangs in the air and there's a cosy prospect of jumpers, or perhaps a spiced, baked apple. This is the season to gather first-frosted sloes for winter gins and berries to make jams that will bring cheer to the dark months. More deeply, *rudenėja* conjures a sense of melancholy - for lost teenage summers, for a sense of time running ever faster - and represents a last chance to warm faces in the sun before the skinny fingers of winter start to grip.

Isblink

(ees-blink)

Swedish, Noun

Navigators have long used natural phenomena to help them chart a safe course to their destination. *Isblink* describes the glowing white light that appears near the Arctic horizon, particularly on the underside of low cloud. This luminous, otherworldly glow indicates the presence of an ice field in the far distance, its stretches of white reflecting the sun's rays up into the atmosphere. Conversely, its counterpart, the dark 'water sky' shows where the more easily traversable stretches of open water lie. The phenomena were used as navigation tools by Norwegian Arctic explorer, Fridtjof Nansen, during his failed 1893 expedition to the North Pole.

Kapel капель

(kar-pyel)

Russian, Noun

Shhhh. Can you hear something... melting? The plop-plop-plop of icicles dripping water is the sound of the sun starting to warm the earth, and thus a sign that the world is thawing. Waking on a bright morning to the plip-plip of drops of water puts the Russian nation into a cheerful mood. An onomatopoeic, crystalline little word, *kapel* or *capelle* (drops) encapsulates that positive feeling that greener, sunnier days are just around the corner and spring has begun.

Chelidonian

(chell-i-donian)

English, Adjective

Chelidon is the Greek word for swallow, the little, fork-tailed bird whose joyous swoops and acrobatic dives mark the start of the UK's spring. For many, the return of these migratory birds is a cause for quietly relieved celebration: nature's clock continues to tick to time, and warmer, lazier days lie ahead. *Chelidonian* winds are those balmy, gentle breezes that accompany the return of these distinctively silhouetted birds, bearing them higher as they perform their graceful airshow in the sky.

Friluftsliv

(free-loofts-liv)

Norwegian, Noun

Many Scandinavians believe that there's no better way to enjoy nature than by immersing yourself in it in a relaxed fashion. *Friluftsliv* translates as 'open-air living' and was a concept popularised by Norwegian writer, Henrik Ibsen, in the 1850s. Today, you might indulge in *friluftsliv* through foraging for berries, taking a wood-fired sauna with friends, or camping next to a lake. It's more about spiritual well-being and traditional recreation than about pure exercise, aiming to win, or taking part in extreme sports. Think of it as a slow enjoyment of the wild, with the focus on the surroundings rather than the activity; a time to nurture the soul as well as the body.

Smeuse

(smee-ooze)

British English, Noun

If a small animal repeatedly uses a path through a hedge or wall, it creates a *smeuse*, a small gap. This word is believed to be related to the Cumbrian word *smoot* (a gap in a drystone wall through which sheep can pass and be counted) and the Middle French word *meuse* (hiding place), but it's more fun to think of it as a combination of sssssssqueeeze and moussssssse. It's a word that, once you're aware of its existence, opens a door to a new little world; these small openings are now added to your rag-bag of sights to spot on an evening walk. Listen for the tell-tale bustle in the hedgerow, look for the *smeuse* and, if you're lucky, you might spy a darting hare, rabbit, water rat or weasel.

Solvarg

(sul-varj)

Swedish, Noun

'Sun dogs' or 'mock suns', also known to scientists as parhelia, are the two hazy glows in the sky that sit each side of the sun. Sometimes they're bright white, but occasionally colourfully splashed with reds and blues. You're most likely to see these rainbow-like orbs when the sun is near the horizon; the phenomenon is caused by ice crystals in the atmosphere that act as tiny, perfect prisms. Across the UK and Scandinavia, they're associated with hounds, and it's been suggested that this springs from a folk memory of the two mythological wolves from Norse mythology who chase the sun and moon: *Sköll* and *Hati Hróðvitnisson*.

Allochthonous

(allock-tho-nus)

English, Adjective

This geological term is used to describe 'different earth'; rocks or sediments that have travelled - sometimes incredibly long distances - from their place of origin. It might describe a huge mountain block heaved into place by enormous tectonic forces, or the smallest grains of sediment that have slowly washed from another shoreline and settled. Rather poetically, these nomadic rocks were defined by 20th-century geologist John Challinor as 'the far-travelled ground'. Uncovering - or imagining - rocks' journeys can bring a different dimension to your wanderings. What awe-inspiring forces have worked together to create the landscape around us? And how might it change in the future?

Aloha ʻĀina

(ar-lo-ha eye-ee-nah)

Hawaiian, Noun

Hawaiian mythology suggests that humans were born to the earth mother and the sky father. This umbilical connection to the natural world is embodied in the concept of *aloha ʻāina* (love of the land). A sense of all aspects of life being intertwined with every living thing, this idea brings the Hawaiians' passion for their country and the wider natural world to politics, religion, science and the community. It's a complex word that particularly relates to the aspects of nature that help maintain life; *ai* means 'to eat', so sustenance is at the heart of the concept. It's become interlaced with politics and particularly nationalism, as well as a social movement that focuses on ecology and peace and more latterly on the growing of kalo, a sacred plant at the heart of Hawaii's culture.

Gribnoy dozhd

Грибной дождь

(grib-noy dosht)

———

Russian, Noun

At the first sign of *Gribnoy dozhd* - a rain that's misty and light, with the sun peeking through the clouds - many Russians make their way to the forest. For this is mushroom weather, the kind of conditions that, people believe, encourage fungi to grow faster and thicker. Mushroom picking is an activity close to the heart of many Russians; the country is home to over 200 different varieties of edible mushrooms. *Gribnoy dozhd* not only describes this gentle, warm rain, but also evokes a sense of nostalgia and wistfulness for foraging expeditions gone by.

Zhaghzhagh زغزغ

(zaaang-zaaar-gh)

Persian, Noun

This word is not just onomatopoeic; the physical act of saying
it betrays its meaning. *Zhaghzhag* is the sound that comes from
chattering teeth, whether that's due to anger or the cold. Shivering
makes teeth chatter; it's an unconscious reflex our body uses to force
movement to warm us when we are chilly. This chittering word also
describes the noise that nuts make when rattled. The Sufi mystic
and poet, Rumi, uses *zhaghzhag* in his epic *Masnavi*, "Were it not for
the sweetness of a kernel's voice, who would listen to the rattling
voice of a walnut-shell?"

Author Biography

Kate Hodges has written eight books that have been translated into eight languages. Her titles include biography collections *Warriors, Witches, Women* and *I Know A Woman*. She has also written guides to London, among them *Little London, Rural London, Welcome to the Dark Side: Occult London* and *London in an Hour*, and family activity books *Rock, Paper, Scissors* and *On a Starry Night*. She writes part-time for The Green Parent Magazine and plays in cult bands The Hare and Hoofe and Ye Nuns. She lives by the sea in Hastings with her 10-year-old twins, Arthur and Dusty.

katehodges.org
instagram.com/theekatehodges
@theekatehodges on Twitter

Acknowledgements

Many thanks to:
Alison Wise, Guri Hummelsund, Keiko Shimmer-Müller, Aina Pastor Barceló, Kati Brugnoli, Elisabeth Kristensen, Malin Hjelte, Monica Ugalde, Megan Green, Doug Taylor, Andy Dunlop, Sophie Davies, Sarra Manning, Chiara Thomas, Paul Phillips, Polly Wilson, Sarah Howlett.

Facebook group The Omnigot Fan Club: Elisabeth Simelton, Natasa Gajic, Xavier Romero-Frias, Lily Pomar, Waruno Mahdi, Casandra Ciocian, Brian Corliss Tawney, Julie Croston, Vesla Mumbul.

Enormous thanks to Yang Sio Maan for her sensitive and charming illustrations that bring this book to life, to Sophie Allen at Pavilion for her genius concept and steady steering hand, to Anne Sheasby for her perceptive copy editing and to Alice Kennedy-Owen for her clever design skills.

As ever, I'm indebted to my agent Juliet Pickering, and Sian Ellis-Martin, Ane Reason and Lizzy Attree at Blake Friedmann.

First published in the United Kingdom in 2021 by
Portico
43 Great Ormond Street
London
WC1N 3HZ

An imprint of Pavilion Books Company Ltd

Copyright © Pavilion Books Company Ltd 2021
Text copyright © Kate Hodges 2021

All rights reserved. No part of this publication may be copied, displayed, extracted,
reproduced, utilised, stored in a retrieval system or transmitted in any form or by
any means, electronic, mechanical or otherwise including but not limited to
photocopying, recording, or scanning without the prior written permission of the
publishers.

ISBN 978-1-911622-71-0

A CIP catalogue record for this book is available from the British Library.
10 9 8 7 6 5 4 3 2 1

Illustrator: Yang Sio Maan
Commissioning editor: Sophie Allen
Design management: Alice Kennedy-Owen
Production manager: Phil Brown

Reproduction by Rival Colour Ltd., London
Printed and bound by Toppan Leefung Printing Ltd., China
www.pavilionbooks.com